Ludwig van Beethoven

COMPLETE PIANO CONCERTOS
in Full Score

Dover Publications, Inc.
New York

Published in Canada by General Publishing Company, Ltd., 30 Lesmill Road, Don Mills, Toronto, Ontario.
Published in the United Kingdom by Constable and Company, Ltd.

This Dover edition, first published in 1983, is an unabridged republication of Nos. 65 through 69 (and part of 70a) of Series 9 ("Für Pianoforte und Orchester") of the collection *Ludwig van Beethoven's Werke; Vollständige kritisch durchgesehene überall berechtigte Ausgabe; mit Genehmigung aller Originalverleger,* originally published by Breitkopf & Härtel, Leipzig, n.d. [1862–65].

Manufactured in the United States of America
Dover Publications, Inc., 31 East 2nd Street, Mineola, N.Y. 11501

Library of Congress Cataloging in Publication Data

Beethoven, Ludwig van, 1770–1827.
  [Concertos, piano, orchestra]
  Complete piano concertos.

  Reprint. Originally published: Leipzig : Breitkopf & Härtel, 1862–1865.
  1. Concertos (Piano)—Scores.
M1010.B41 1983   83-5169
ISBN 0-486-24563-2

Contents

NOTE: Not included here are three additional cadenzas for Op. 58 that were not published until 1959–1971.

Piano Concerto No. 1 in C Major, Op. 15

RONDO.

Piano Concerto No. 2 in B-flat Major, Op. 19

84   CONCERTO NO. 2 IN B-FLAT MAJOR

Piano Concerto No. 3 in C Minor, Op. 37

muta in C.

Trombe.

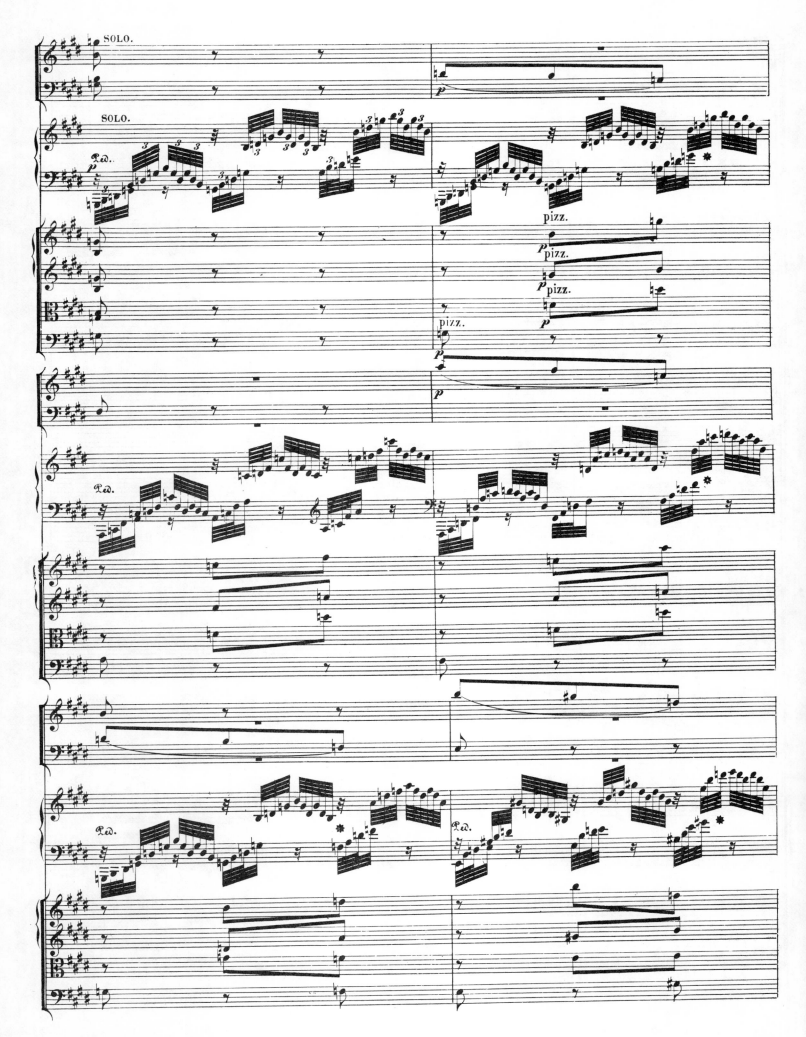

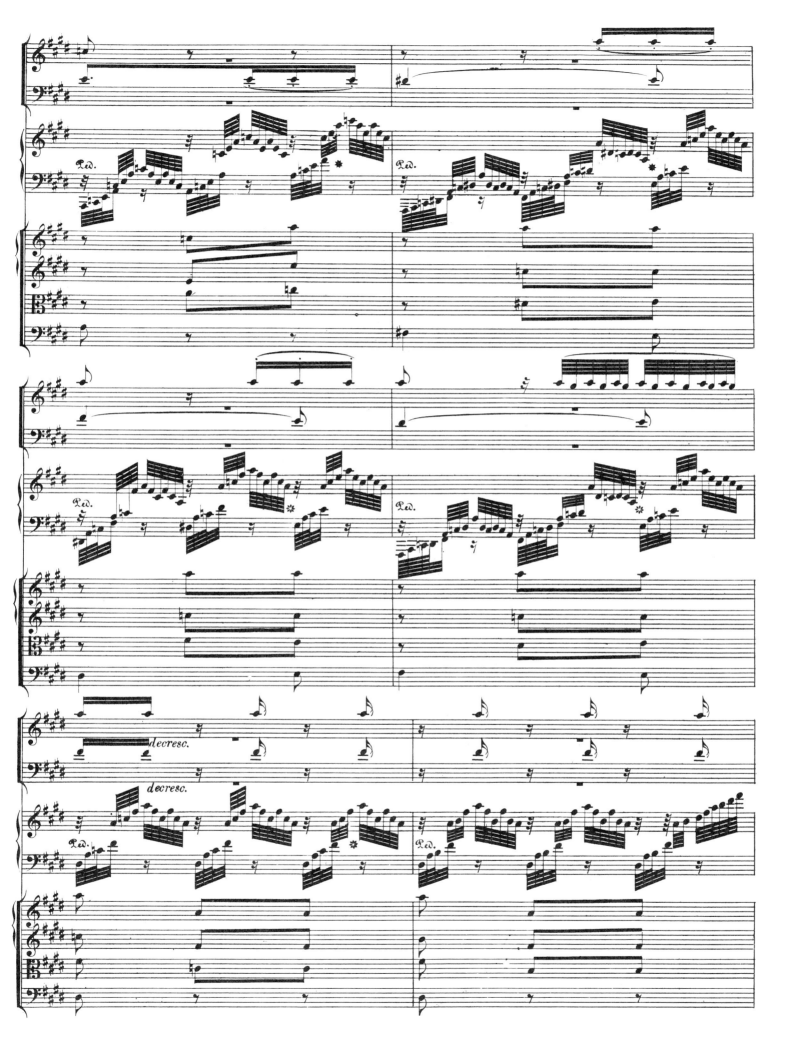

RONDO.

Allegro.

SOLO.

Flauti.

Oboi.

Clarinetti in B.

Fagotti.

Corni in Es.
(poi in C.)

Trombe in C.

Timpani in C.G.

Allegro.

Pianoforte.

Allegro.

Violino I.

Violino II.

Viola.

Bassi.

Ob.

Fag.

Cor.

pizz.

pizz.

pizz.

pizz.

Piano Concerto No. 4 in G Major, Op. 58

*) During the entire Andante the pianist must use the soft pedal (*una corda*) uninterruptedly; the mark "Ped." is an additional reference to the occasional use of the ordinary pedal.

262   Concerto No. 4 in G Major

Piano Concerto No. 5 in E-flat Major, Op. 73
("Emperor")

NB. Non si fa una Cadenza, ma s'attacca subito il seguente.

RONDO.

Cadenzas

Concerto No. 1, First Movement (1)

(continuation
missing)

Concerto No. 1, First Movement (2)

dolce

Concerto No. 1, First Movement (3)

Concerto No. 2, First Movement

Concerto No. 3, First Movement

Poco meno allegro e risoluto.

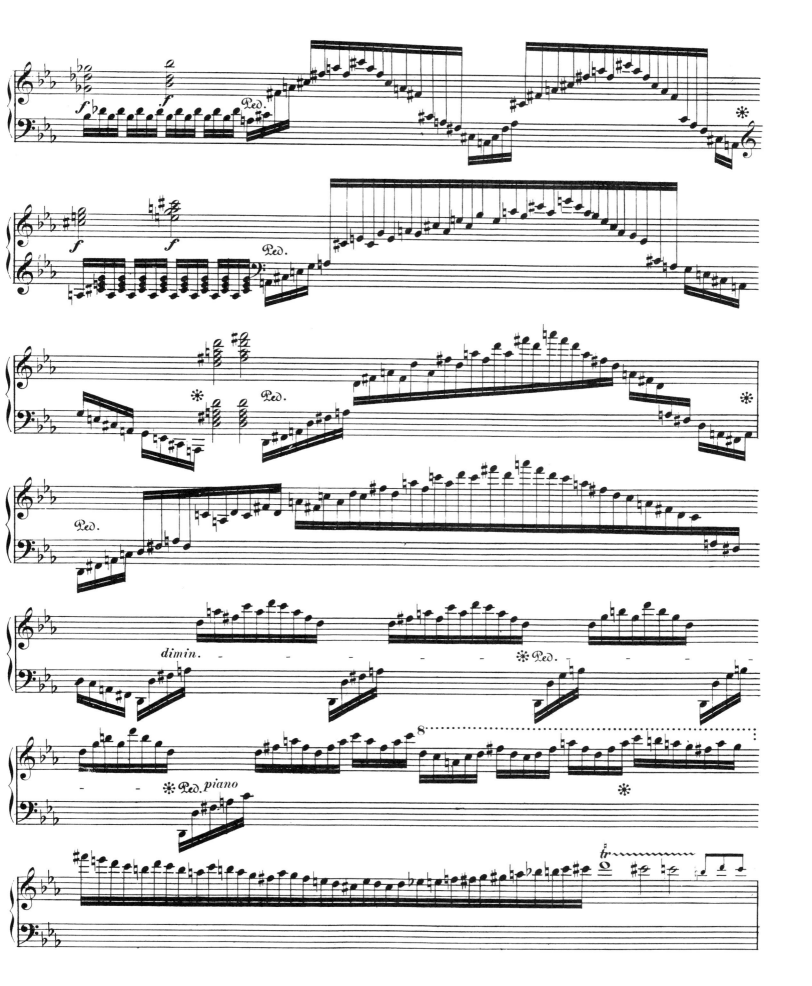

Concerto No. 4, First Movement (1)

Tempo primo.

Concerto No. 4, First Movement (2)

Concerto No. 4, Third Movement

[END OF VOLUME.]